SILKIES: EVERYTHING YOU WANT TO KNOW ABOUT THE FLUFF-BALLS

First Printing, 2021

ISBN 978-0-9926048-1-3

PIB Publishing
13 Pencross View
Hemyock
Cullompton
Devon. EX15 3XH
United Kingdom

Table of Contents

Chapter 1: Introduction

Silkies chickens are one of the most intriguing chickens I have ever had a chance to read about. They go with various names; fluff-balls, the Chinese silk chickens, or Silky. Their name comes from their silk/satin-like feathers. Silkies are a wonderful breed with an interesting way of interacting with humans.

Silky chickens are one of the most playful chickens. They are quite affectionate and they are known for their friendly temperament. Silkies are typically calm in nature and make wonderful pets for homes and especially for families that have children. They can be a great pet for your backyard. It has been popularly seen that silkies can be extremely affectionate with their owners if they give them sufficient time and handle them with care as well.

Silkies are not only beautiful but they also have some amazing traits. This book will give you a comprehensive overview of this incredible breed of chicken.

If you are thinking of getting a Chinese silk chicken or if you are a new owner to one, then this book is perfect for you. It will help you in understanding and learning everything you need to know about the silkies. This book will explore various topics related to this wonderful breed of chicken. It will also touch upon the history of silkies and the questions that commonly arise in the minds of new owners.

In addition to this, this book will guide the new owners in deciding which silkie they should get and how they can set up their coop. There are certain needs of silkies that must be fulfilled and you will learn all those needs in the coming chapters. Along with it, you will also be provided with a guideline as to how you can look after the silkies.

Whenever we get a new pet, we must always familiarize ourselves with its anatomy. You should know their various physical features and the varieties that can be found within this breed. When we become a new parent to a baby, we are always so cautious of what they can eat and what they cannot eat. Similarly, when you become an owner of a silkie, you should first learn about the foods your silkie can or cannot eat. Not only this but there are certain ways or tips you should follow while feeding them. This book will help you in understanding all of this.

Additionally, the book will explore serious topics such as possible illnesses for the silkies chickens, the diseases and the precautions owners should take. Understandably, these topics are scary for the owners but they must learn about them in order to prevent such things from happening.

By the end of this book, you will learn about the laying and breeding process of silkies. It will involve topics such as mating, hatchlings, and how you can then feed the silkie chicks.

Thus, if you are looking for a book that can give you everything you want to know about the silkies chickens, then you don't have to look anymore. This is the perfect one for you. By the end of this book, you will know everything you need to know about the silkies as the new owner or if you are planning on getting one.

Chapter 2: The Silkies: Things You Want to Know

It is highly important to get to know the chicken you are planning to own or if you already own but don't know much about. Before going into an in-depth discussion about the important things you should know about raising and breeding them, let's first go over the basics of what silkies are.

There are many of you who picked this book up because you never really heard about this breed of chicken or seen one. So, this chapter is going to introduce you to this incredible bird that is known for its interesting appearance, friendly nature, and reputation as a brooder.

The pictures in this book will instantly make you fall in love with this beautiful chicken. However, the pictures don't tell the entire story as to what silkies really are and the information you need in order to completely understand this breed. This chapter will help you in understanding the history of silkies, along with the common questions that might arise in someone's mind who is new to this breed.

1. What is the Silkie?

As mentioned earlier, silkies have various names. Some call them silkies chicken, while some call them Chinese chicken. And then there are some who can't resist its beauty and call it a fluff-ball. Essentially, they are a breed of chicken that is identified by its feathers. They have soft, satin like feathers that have a silky touch to them. Hence, there is where the name comes from.

Silky resembles a puffball due to their fur like feathers. These birds are generally friendly and sweet, and they make great pets for anyone who keeps them in their home. You know when you want to cuddle your pet but don't know if you should since they are chicken? Well, silkies are the chicken you can cuddle as they are complacent and enjoy the love and affection from their owners.

Silkies are usually tamed and very easy to handle by everyone. They are also friendly to children and this is one of the reasons why they make an incredible pet. Essentially, silkies are ornamental chickens. They do lay eggs, however, it is not as frequent as the other breeds of chicken. As a matter of fact, Silkies chicken only lays eggs between 90 to 120 eggs per year.

There are three different varieties of silkie chickens;
1. The bearded
2. Non-bearded
3. Bantam

The silkie chicken is adored by many people mainly for its unusual appearance. They are the unique ones in the world of chickens as they are the only breed to have such furry feathers.

Silkies have a long history, which will be discussed in the coming part of this book. However, to touch upon the topic, the history goes back to the Chinese dynasties, eastern Europe, and the Atlantic to modern-day America. Silkies have become one of the most adored chickens by so many people around the world.

2. The Background of the Silkie

Before diving deep into the history of the Silkie chicken, it should be mentioned that the origin of this bird is not known. However, there are some traces that can be found upon investigating the history, that can give us some idea as to where it came from and the places it has traveled to.

The history of silkies runs back to Ancient China when the silkies first appeared.

One thing is certain in its origin, silkies come from somewhere in Southeast Asia. It is also speculated that they may have come from either India or Java.

Silkies first appeared in the documentation form when they were mentioned in one of the works of Marco Polo in the 13th century when he wrote about furry chickens. In his piece, he wrote that he came across this specific breed of chicken during his travels through Asia. One of the naturalists at the University of Bologna named Ulissa Aldorvandi described this breed in one of his pieces when he published a treatise on chickens.

It has popularly been believed by many that silkies were imported to many countries through the Silk Route. However, it is still unknown as to how they made their way into Europe and North America.

The silkies chicken were officially recognized by North America by 1984. They were accepted in the Standard of Perfect and then became a very common breed in Western Europe and North America.

In contemporary times, this beautiful breed is still raised and adored as an ornamental breed. However, they do lay eggs and breed which will be discussed in detail in the coming chapters of this book.

3. Commonly Asked Questions about Silkies

There are multiple questions that might have come to your mind regarding silkies, and in this section of the book, I'll try to address all of those questions that are frequently asked by the new owners or the ones who are intrigued by this magnificent chicken.

1. What bird are silkies?

Silkies are chickens. They are bantam, meaning that they were not bred selectively from larger birds. The origin of silkies is unknown but the records highlight that they have been around for a long time and come from somewhere in Southeast Asia.

2. Are silkies capable of flying?

No, silkies cannot fly like other birds. This is because of the structure of their feathers. According to their anatomy, their wings are not capable of holding air in order to carry them.

3. How frequently do silkies lay an egg?

Silkies don't lay eggs as frequently as the other chickens. They are essentially ornamental chickens and that is why they are considered poor layers. Silkies only give about two to three eggs per week.

4. Why do silkies have furry fuzzy feathers?

The reason silkies are fuzzy is that they do not have the cartilage material which is found between the individual strands of "hair" on the shaft of feathers. This cartilage material is known as Barbicels and acts as microscopic "hooks" that are used to hold each hair together. Said barbicels are responsible for giving the shape of "hard feather". Silkies lack those barbicels, henceforth, the individual hairs on their feathers fly free, and as a result, they appear as fur.

5. Do silkies make good free-ranging birds?

As a matter of fact, silkies do not make good free ranging birds. The reason lies in the fact that they cannot fly and can easily become vulnerable to any attacks. They are often prone to become the target of prey animals such as hawks, dogs, and rodents. When under attack, it becomes highly difficult for them to effectively escape from other prey animals.

6. Are silkies good pets?
The temperament of silkies is quite docile and friendly. This makes them exceptionally great pets for homeowners and families with children. When they are given a chance to interact with their owners regularly, they sometimes learn to follow them around as other pets do such as dogs.

7. How many colors do silkies come in?

Interestingly, silkies come in eight recognized colors.

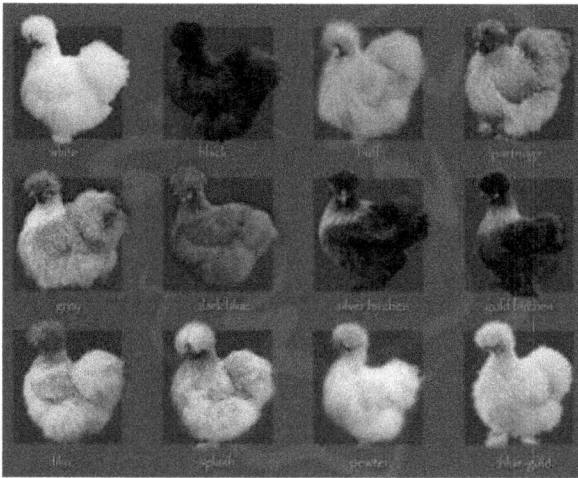

I. Black
II. Blue
III. Buff
IV. Gray
V. Partridge
VI. Self-blue
VII. Splash
VIII. White

8. What color eggs do silkies lay?

Silkies chickens lay eggs in white or cream color with occasional tinting.

9. Can silkies see?

Silkies can see. However, their vision is not as good as the other birds. The reason behind this is, they have large crests known as "top knots" that sometimes impair their vision. Birds that have smaller top knots are capable of seeing better than the birds who have larger top knots. This also contributes to the fact that silkies become more vulnerable to attacks from prey as they cannot see very well.

10. At what age can you sex a silkie?

One of the most asked questions related to silkies is the debate and confusion surrounding the correct age of sexing a silkie. Silkies are considered to be one of the hardest breeds to sex until they are six months old or more. Even when they are at the age of six months, it becomes difficult to guess if they really are ready for sexing. It has been seen, breeders who have raised silkies for more than decades also indicate that it is almost impossible to accurately sex a silkie until they are at least six months old.

11. How do silkies react to cold weather or during winters?

Silkies react the same way towards winters as any other hard feathered breeds. They can easily tolerate it and do not require any special accommodations or preparations other than what you would typically provide to the other birds. Although you might think that they have differently shaped feathers than other birds, still they can keep themselves warm.

12. How are silkies as mothers?

Silkies are exceptionally good mothers. In fact, they are considered to be one of the best poultry mothers around. It has been said that silkies would try to hatch a door knob if they are given the chance. They are also used to naturally hatch out birds such as quail and other non-broody poultry breeds.

These are one of the most frequently asked questions about the silkies chickens. If you still have more questions, then don't worry. This book will explore everything that is related to silkies and by the end of this book, you will know everything you want to learn and all your questions will have been answered.

Chapter 3: A Beginner's Guide to the New Owners

You are probably experiencing a very exciting time right now. You might have already purchased a silkie or planning on getting one and bringing it to your home and family. However, it can be extremely overwhelming at first because you have no idea which one to get and how to look after them.

It is understandable, whenever we become a new parent, that time is quite exciting. You want to take the baby home but you are also overwhelmed and worried about the prospect of looking after the newly born baby. Getting a new pet also makes you a new parent. You can't wait to spend time with it, feed it and look after it but you are also worried, what if you take one wrong step and what if you wouldn't be able to figure it out? However, it is difficult at first to get a hang of it, but with the passage of time, you observe, understand, and learn everything.

This chapter is going to help you with it. First, you will learn about getting the silkie, which one to get, and if you will be able to raise them. Then, this chapter will provide you with a complete guideline as to how you can set up a coop for them and the things silkies will need once they are settled.

By the end of this chapter, you will also learn about the pros and cons of owning a silkie. Sometimes, we get a pet in an impulsive decision without pondering up the current circumstances and if we are capable of raising it and giving it the time and care it deserves.

1. *Which Ones to Get?*

It can be very exhausting to decide which silkie to purchase, especially when you have no prior knowledge about this breed.

One of the first confusions comes from the fact that you are not sure where to go in order to purchase it. Silkies are often not readily available at the local breeder's. They mostly sell those chickens that lay eggs or sell chicken meat. Whereas, silkies are an ornamental breed and this makes it difficult to find them.

Nonetheless, you should not immediately let this scare you into giving up on the idea of buying a silkie. There are still many sources from which you can purchase one for yourself. You can look for a silkie chicken online on various platforms that sell poultry. eBay can be one of the options. However, you should also first consult the local market or the silkie club in your town as they can guide you in from where to get one.

Before going into all the troubles of finding a silkie breeder, first, take some time to find out about the laws in your area. There are some areas that do not allow keep chickens in the homes. Also, you might have to get a permit to keep one in your backyard. Some areas require permits while there are some that have a complete ban on keeping a chicken in backyards. Hence, check the laws first and then plan about getting a silkie for your home.

If your area allows it and you want to start searching for the silkie breeder, then keep this essential information in your mind. When you are looking for a breeder, be very careful. There are some silkie breeders in the market that are crossing silkies with other breeds. This can affect the type of feather that you get. Thus, make sure that you are purchasing from a breeder of purebred silkies.

Additionally, there is one thing that should always be considered while purchasing a silkie. You should at least buy three silkies at one time. The reason behind this is, silkies are sociable chickens and they enjoy being in a flock. A single silkie will probably become lonely and consequently, this will affect her health and lifespan.

Moreover, before going to the silkie breeder, you should ponder upon whether you wish to purchase young adults silkie, a chick and raise it on your own, or if you want to bring home eggs and then watch it hatch and then raise it. You can do any of these aforementioned things but do not impulsively take a decision without reading about them and familiarizing yourself with silkies.

Raising a chicken can be a delight and exciting for you, but it can be quite loud and when you are living in an area such as the suburbs, you should make sure that your neighbors don't have any problems with it. Otherwise, it can later give birth to many conflicts. So, check with your neighbors and try to maintain as much peace with them as you can.

All these aforementioned tips should be kept under consideration while getting a silkie. Once you have got one, and you bring it home. You want to make it as much comfortable for them as possible. So, the next step is about setting up a coop for the silkies.

2. Setting Up a Coop for the Silkies

Generally speaking, silkies are low-maintenance chickens. They don't require extra efforts or things in the coop, than the other breeds of chicken. However, due to some reasons, they do have slightly different requirements when it comes to housing them. It is clear that silkies are different from the other breeds of chickens in a multiple way. Such differences can be seen in setting up a specific coop for the silkies or purchasing one for them.

Silkies themselves are not very demanding. Their docile nature reflects in this as well. They can be happy in a small coop and only require about two square feet of space per chicken. Although this is enough space for them to roam around and rest comfortably, still it is recommended that silkies should be provided with more room than only two square feet of space.

Silkies are essentially ornamental chickens. They are popularly used by many for Silkie shows and thus it is highly important to protect their feathers from any kind of damage. This is why they should be given more room. Moreover, you can also let them roam around in your backyard. But it should be mentioned here that silkies are extremely vulnerable to any kind of prey attacks. Henceforth, if left to range free, they should be constantly under supervision and the owner should protect them from any fly preys.

There are certain traits a coop for any breed of chicken should have.

Safety:

This is the general rule of thumb; a coop must provide safety to the silkies. A safety from not only the attack of prey but also from the harsh weather. It should be kept in an area that does not give any way to the predators to reach the coop or the silkies chickens.

In addition to this, the coop should be built in a way that provides complete protection from winds and restrains rain and snow from damaging the coop or the silkies. Coops do not have to be insulated. Nonetheless, if you feel the need to insulate your coop, then you should seal it into the walls. Pecking the insulation could make the silkies get sick.

Moreover, make the coop draft free. A good coop for silkies must have walls and a solid roof. Silkies can tolerate any kind of weather, as mentioned earlier, but the feathers of silkies are not like other chickens' feathers. The water will not run off their backs. Hence, the coop must protect them from rain, wind, and too much sun.

Fencing:

An owner should always make sure that there is fencing around the run. The run is the outside yard where the chickens can be outside and scratch. The fence should be high enough in order to prevent the silkies chickens from jumping out. Generally, silkies do not jump high but they can jump about three to four feet in the air. However, there is always a danger of a predator and that is why the fence should be high enough to protect the silkies from the attack.

Moreover, another thing is also essential, you should place a hardware cloth in the ground. The said cloth should attach to the bottom of the fence and it goes twelve inches into the ground. This technique is done in order to prevent the predators from attacking the silkies chickens by going under the fence.

In addition to this, you should also keep under the consideration the age of your chickens for whom you are building this fence. The size of the fence must align with their age. To elaborate further, chicks require chick size fencing, while on the other hand, chickens can use any type of fencing.

Silkies cannot fly that is why they do not require a large area. However, if provided them with the opportunity to roam around after being enclosed, they become happier and consequently healthier. Provide an enclosed chicken run where the silkies can scratch for seeds, bugs, and other such items. It can be about four square feet area per bantam silkie and eight to ten square feet for heavier silkies.

Lighting:

One of the most important things that must be kept under consideration while setting up a coop for silkies is proper lighting. When a coop lacks proper lighting, that affects the laying process for the chickens. Insufficient light results in chicken stop laying eggs or the process slows down during the months of winters.

Chickens thrive on roaming around in an open area. That is why you should also focus on offering them fresh air and sunshine.

Another thing that goes hand in hand with lighting is heat lamps. In places that are quite cold during winters, you should add a heat lamp to the coop in order to provide sufficient warmth during the cold weather. However, you should keep the lamp to the side so that the chickens can move away from the heat and don't get damaged.

Ventilation:

Good ventilation is not only important for humans but it is equally important for the chickens. There are multiple understandable reasons, however, one of the most important reasons is that the chickens dropping contain quite a large amount of ammonia in them. This ammonia can become a cause of respiratory problems in the silkies. Thus, it is very essential for the coop to have ventilation.

Nesting Boxes:

Nesting boxes can be purchased and can also be built. Many coops come with nesting boxes already attached to them. however, if you plan on building one, then you can use cola crates for them since the silkies will lay eggs and nest.

Roost Poles:

Generally, it is believed that silkies do not roost, however, as some time passes, they do start to perch and roost. However, they do not roost as frequently as the other breed of chickens. But you can set a roost in their coops but it should be about 16 inches high, maximum since silkies cannot jump high and it is the highest they can jump. When it comes to how apart the roost poles should be, consider putting them one foot apart in order to give each bird about one foot to roost on.

3. Everything the Silkies Will Need

Silkies have certain needs that need to be fulfilled when you are housing them. Just like any other pets, they also require few supplies which are used for the purpose of providing them as much comfort as you can. Such supplies are;

Feed:

Nutrition is quite important for the silkies chickens. This is why it is fundamental to provide your silkies with an excellent quality commercial feed. Some breeders make their own feed, however, it is recommended that silkies should be given a commercially formulated feed.

Waterer:

You should purchase the kind of waterer that hangs so you would not have as many shavings, feces, and dirt in the waterer. When it comes to waterers, go for the ones that have 96 inches of trough space for hundred birds. One waterer is enough if you have two or three silkies. That will keep them hydrated.

Feeder:

The feeder is equally important as the waterer. It is purposely designed to feed dishes for chickens. It hangs and is up off of the ground. One feeder is enough for two or three birds. In addition to this, you want the one with three hundred inches of through space for every hundred birds.

Bedding:

Bedding is an essential element in every nest box. It is recommended that owners should opt for the pine shaving ones since they are used in the prevention of pest infestations as much as other bedding. You can also use hay and stray for bedding for the silkies chickens.

Sand:

Sand is used as a dust bath by the birds. It should be used by the silkies on daily basis. You can either place the sand in a dry spot in your run or you can also put it into a bucket that is used by silky to get into.

Grit:

Grits are small stones, shells, and gravel that chickens swallow to grind up the food properly that they are provided. If the chickens are given the opportunity to roam around and range free, then the owner does not have to provide them as much grit because they will pick stones on their own. However, if the silkies do not put them up themselves or they do not have the access to the grit, then you much have a supply for them.

4. Pros and Cons of Owning a Silkie Chicken

You have started thinking of getting a silkie. This time is exciting but you might be slightly confused as well. You are not sure if you want to get one or not. The silkies chickens look cute, funny, so cuddly, and adorable. But there are so many things one should know about them before deciding on whether to get one or not. Before you purchase one or invest in one, make sure that you know about the pros and cons of owning a silkie.

In the previous sections of this chapter, you learned about which one you should get and how to purchase a silkie. The next sections discussed the essentials of setting up a coop for your new fluffy pet and everything it would probably need. But you should also familiarize yourself with the positives and negatives factors involving in owning a silkie. So, let's start discussing them so you shall know if you are ready to purchase one or not.

Pros:

- Silkies make great pets. It has already been established that they are great with owners, families, and children. They are fluffy, lovable, and cute. They quickly learn to live with humans and start acting friendly.

- This pro goes hand in hand with the one mentioned above. Silkies are quite fluffy and each of their feathers is fluttering and flying. This makes them really nice for petting.
- Silkie chickens make excellent broody hens and sitters. They are determined sitters and will hatch Guinea fowl and duck eggs. The eggs need 28 to 35 days of incubation.
- Silkies chickens are quiet. This makes them great in the neighborhood of suburban areas, where you can keep them in the backyard coop. the cockerels have a soft and quiet crow and the hens even make much less noise than any other breed. This can be very helpful for the owners especially considering that how difficult it becomes to keep chickens in some areas.
- One of the least talked about pros of keeping a silkie chicken is that they can be kept in an apartment. Obviously, considering the fact that you are allowed to keep one according to the building laws. Silkies are not very fond of muddy places or getting wet. This is why it is easy to keep them in an apartment.
- The eggs of silkies are quite delicious. Even though they are small but they are also really nice and have good strong shells and bight yolks.
- Silkies cannot fly nor they can hop very high. This is one of the reasons why they are easy to be kept in the backyard.
- Silkie chickens are low maintenance. They do not require extravagant food items or maintenance things. They are generally petite, thrifty, and lightweight birds and they like to free-range. This can mean that they are inexpensive to keep.

- Silkies chickens are great parents. Hens are good mothers to their chicks and the roosters are also great dads.
- They are great with kids. Their nature is docile and not at all aggressive. Silkies are quite passive and not flappy type and this makes them of incredible pets. Silkies are a very friendly breed. They appreciate the attention of their owners. They also enjoy the company of children. In addition to that, they like to play with children.

Cons:

- Although the feathers look so beautiful, they do not protect silkies chickens from the rain and snow, they can get wet through easily. This can consequently make this breed cold.

As it has already been mentioned, silkies are highly vulnerable to attacks from predators. They can easily be killed by them due to their decreased vision and size.

This is why they require constant supervision if they are left to free range. Otherwise, their coop must be built in a way that can ensure protection to them from any kind of land or air predator.

- Silkie chickens have been known to lay comparatively quite infrequently than the other breeds. They lay around 100 to 120 eggs a year, which is clearly not a big number of eggs per year. Their eggs are also small and you can end up with many egg-less days. Henceforth, if you want to produce more eggs, then you should consider purchasing a different breed because silkies are primarily ornamental chickens.
- Silkies' passive nature can be adorable for humans but it can result in them getting attacked easily. They are too passive to

avoid dangers. Not only because of their docile temperament but also because of the large crests they cannot see as wide an area. This can make them feel relaxed and they fail to recognize the danger until it is too late for them.

- Silkies tend to get messy quickly in muddy ground or wet places. The feathered feet also get messy and it is hard to keep them clean as their anatomy of furs is different than the other breeds.
- It is extremely difficult to determine the sex of silkies. These birds are impossible to sex when they are young. It has been said that you can't determine it even if they are six months old and even when they are older, it can turn out to be difficult.
- Silkies chickens are a fragile breed. They have multiple genetic issues like vaulted skulls that come with the feathers and inbreeding. They are also prone to several diseases, which will be discussed later on in this book. They can also have vitamin deficiencies.
- Silkies chickens do not perch high to sleep. Considering if there are multiple silkies in the coop and they all pile up to sleep at night, that can create problems. However, they can be trained to perch high.

- Silkies can be very trusting and nice and this can create many problems for them. One of those problems is that they can get bullied by other breeds.

This can make them peck the last in order. And when it comes to making their vision a little better, you can trim the feathers that cover their eyes and affect their eyesight. So, they can see clearly and also peck as the other breeds do.

- Silkies have fluffy feathers, which look beautiful. But they also mean that they could host mites and lice, which could become a problem for you and the chickens.
- The feathers tend to get wet easily and do not have the capability to dry off quickly, which can make them very cold during the winters. Similarly, during hot weather, the feathers can make them susceptible to heat-related problems as well.
- It has been said by various silkies chickens' owners that the silkies are one of the rarest breeds that can starve themselves to death on a nest. They go broody quite often and this can become self-destructive on their part.

- All silkies have extra toes. They can sometimes have one or two at least, which can create problems for them.
- Silkies are one of the rarest breeds and this could mean that they are also expensive to buy. If you are looking for a cheap investment in chickens that can provide you eggs on a regular basis, then silkies are not the right choice for you. However, if you want to invest in an expensive bird and raise it for the shows then you can go for silkies.

Silkies are gentle and kind birds. They love to have company and they are fond of being held and cared for. They thrive for the attention of their owners. They are generally low maintenance, however, there are certain requirements of keeping a silkie healthy that need to be fulfilled.

This chapter dived deep into the factors that involved in purchasing the silkies chickens and the things they will need once you buy them. By now, you have also probably learned how to set a coop for them that contains every essential item and the list of pros and cons of owning them. this guide has probably helped you in deciding whether to get one or not and if you have already purchased one, then this chapter should have helped you in understanding the basics. Later in this book, you will learn more information needed in raising these beautiful birds.

Chapter 4: A Guide to Looking After the Silkies

The previous chapter gave you the guidelines as to how you can set a coop for your silkies and the things they will need. If you have already gotten yourself this beautiful bird, then you must be wondering about its daily care and how you can look after them.

You should not immediately overwhelm yourself with all these worries and thoughts. Instead, I would suggest that you should enjoy your time with the silkies chickens. Watch them, admire their beauty as they can be really entertaining to look at.

Silkies are generally very social and adaptable. They are not only beautiful in the pictures but also magnificent when they roam around and play in the backyard on the coop. Their personality is quite enjoyable and they can easily make the humans around them fond of this bird.

However, in the excitement of getting the silkies, you should not forget that they also need their own space. You should not make them feel enclosed or crowded. This also indicates that each silkie must be given its required space in the coop. The silkie house must only be reserved for two or three chickens at the time and not the entire large amount of flock. Each of the chickens should be given two square feet of space per every silkie in the coop.

In the early days of bringing your silkies home and letting them get settled on their own in the hen house, you will start to notice that silkies have a tendency to place their own order in pecking when they are in a flock. This is not something unusual for them. however, as it has been mentioned earlier as well, silkies can get picked on easily. They have a very nice and trusting nature and this could make them become last in the pecking order. If you notice bullying for several days in a row, then you should definitely do something about it.

Silkies are very docile and they get along easily with each other. They are not big on fights or getting into trouble, and although, this nature of silkies is excellent when it comes to them interacting with humans and children, this could also become problematic for them as they can easily be bullied by other chickens. This is why it is recommended that silkies should not be kept in a flock of mixed breeds.

When it comes to looking after the silkies, you should follow certain steps. Silkies chickens are generally low maintenance chickens. They don't require much effort but there are a few steps that need to be taken in order to ensure their well-being.

1. Silkies Daily Care

On the daily basis, there are some small steps that go into the care of silkies. They are essential and you should keep them in mind before getting this bird or immediately after getting one.

i.   Keep the waterer clean and wash it out daily.

ii. Fill them with fresh water. In addition to that, add half a cup for Apple Cider Vinegar.

iii. Keep replacing the water for the fresh one and keep checking it multiple times a day. Make the water readily available for the chickens as they can easily get dehydrated.

iv. If it is deemed necessary, replace the dust bath too.

v.   Regularly add grit to the feeder of grit.

vi. Regularly fill the feeders with the feed. Keep checking it and keep checking on the silkies whether they are getting the feed or not.

vii.	Keep the coop clean and remove any kind of dirty straw. Keep checking it for anything that could make the silkies sick.
viii.	Let out the chickens to free range either into the run or the backyard. But keep an eye on them so that no predator could attack or harm them.
ix.	Pick the feeders at night.
x.	Thoroughly wash and clean the feeders and waterers and then let them dry completely.
xi.	If your silkies were out in the yard all day, don't forget to put them back into the coop for the night and check the lock.
xii.	Clean the coop of silkies thoroughly at least once a month.
xiii.	The old bedding needs to be removed to avoid any illnesses.
xiv.	When you clean the coop, spray the floor with a solution of bleach and water.
xv.	When the floor is completely dry, spread fresh pine shavings on the floor.
xvi.	Although it will be discussed in detail in the later chapters of this book, you should check your silkies every week for mites and lice. Keep an eye on pests on your silkies, and if found any, use a pest-control spray on them. spray it again in a week.
xvii.	Keep the environment clean in order to avoid any kind of potential illnesses in the chickens.

For the daily care of silkies, these were all the necessary steps you should follow. On the whole, the care is easy and all you have to do is keep a check on their feed and water throughout the day and look out for any kind of lurking danger in face of predators.

Other things that you need to take off are washing off any feces in the nesting areas and sweeping up the feathers. They are infrequent in laying the eggs, thus it differs from owner to owner. You can collect the eggs once a day or several times a day, depending on the frequency of laying.

When it comes to looking after the silkies as the owners and developing a strong relationship with them, there are a few tips you can follow.

Show affection:

Silkies are very easy to deal with. They enjoy affection and welcome it happily. Silkies are also very easy to tame and they enjoy being handled. You should start handling them and holding them from the very beginning. The more you show them affection, the tamer they will be.

This goes a long way. Silkies become habitual of being handled and this can turn out to be very helpful when you want to check them for any illnesses, mites/lice, or pests. This can also be helpful for them to get well acquainted with your family and they have a tendency to follow around their owners like the other pets.

Provide security:

Provide absolute security to your silkies. Keep checking the coop and run, keep checking it for any signs of wear and tears. Check for any kind of hole in the fence that could provide a way out for the silkies. If you find any, fix it immediately so that they do not wander away and get attacked by any predators.

Silkies can be highly vulnerable and predators can take advantage of a weak fence. They can attack the silkies even when they are inside the coop. So, it is always recommended to keep an eye on that.

You should also place a hardware cloth around your fence and keep a weekly check on it. In order to place it, bury half-inch hardware cloth for about 12 inches below the run of the fence of silkies. This will give an extra security and prevent predators from digging under the fence. After placing it, keep checking the cloth to make sure no digging has been done. Predators can be persistent and they will dig down and pry up the said cloth.

Be mindful of your silkies nutrition:

This will be discussed in detail in this book. However, it is a very useful tip, you should give silkies some treats. It will contribute to their nutritional values and they will also become fonder of you. But also keep in mind that you should not spoil them too much. Nonetheless, a little treat here and there never harms anyone.

Keep the flock the same age:

As it was recommended earlier in this book, when you purchase a silkie, always get two or three at the same time. A lonely silkie could become depressed and consequently, they can become ill. That's why it is always better to keep them in the flock. But you should also give priority to the fact that every chicken in the flock should be of the same age. This can help you in looking after all of them and it could help with the feeding.

Moreover, older chickens tend to bully the younger ones or the smaller, weaker members of the flock. Chickens of the same age do not fight as much and they also do not take advantage of each other's vulnerability.

Similarly, try to keep them in a flock of silkies only. Silkies are friendly and very kind and together, they don't bully the weaker ones. However, other breeds and bigger in not only physiology but also they are smarter. Silkies are usually a daft breed and keeping them in their own breed is easier than keeping them with mixed ones.

This will also mean that there will be fewer injuries and fights amongst them.

Enjoy your time with silkies:

Do not stress yourself out and don't get overwhelmed. Focus on enjoying your time with silkies. Owning a silkie does not mean that you only have them for the purpose of raising and taming. They are your pet and they enjoy the company of their owners. Silkies are very affectionate and easy to handle.

Instead of fussing over providing all the necessities to them, take some time out to enjoy your time with this amazing bird. Play with them, watch them or spoil them. treat them like you would treat any other pet. Make them a part of your family and spend time with them.

Silkies are very low maintenance chickens. Doing all these small things can make them live happy and healthy. Look after them and provide daily care. In no time, you will start enjoying their company more than they will yours.

Chapter 5: Get to Know Your Silkie

Silkie chicken is an Asian bird that makes a great pet. It has a stunning appearance and gentle nature. We have been discussing many traits and characteristics of silkies in the previous chapters.

You are probably now familiar with the basic daily care of silkies. However, it is highly essential for the owners of silkies to get to know the physical features and varieties of this magnificent bird.

You might be thinking, what could be the reason behind learning the anatomy and types of silkies. When you know your pet and understand all its basic features, then it becomes easier for you to look after them and their health.

Several topics will be discussed in this chapter. First, we will cover the anatomy and all the physical features of the silkies chickens. Moving forward, you will learn about the varieties of silkies and sexing this breed.

1. The Anatomy of the Silkies

The anatomy of chickens can be quite complex. It becomes difficult to comprehend it, once we dive deep into it. This is why you only need to understand the anatomy of silkies right now. This chapter will break down the features of silkies that make them a different and unique breed from the other breeds of chicken.

2. Physical Features of the Silkies

i. Feathers:

The feathers of silkies are one of their most prominent features. They have magnificent feathers all over their body, unlike any other breed of chicken.

Other breeds of chicken have very defined feathers, whereas, the feathers of silkies appear to be like the fur of some mammal and not the feathers we are accustomed to looking at. This is one of the reasons many people call silkies *fluff-ball*.

Because of these fur-like feathers, silkies are also easy to handle and hold. They feel soft in our hands and cute at the same time.

Although the feathers do appear different, still they function the same way other chicken feathers do.

Feathers of silkies provide them protection from various elements such as hot or cold weather, however, they do not provide added protection. As it has been mentioned earlier, the feathers of silkies cannot contain air in them, that's why it is highly recommended to protect them from getting wet during rainy weather or snow. It is also better if they don't play in the mud.

One of the features of silkies that is distinct from other breeds of chickens is that they cannot fly nor can they jump high. The feathers are beautiful but they don't help in flying even for short distances.

Upon looking at a single chicken feather, you will find thick hairs growing on either side of the main shaft. These hairs are known as barbs. In most of the feathers, the barbs appear to be straight and neat. When you observe these barbs, you will see that these barbs branch into things called barbules.

Said barbules are aligned with small hooks which are known as barbicels. Those barbicels essentially act like Velcro and they play their role in keeping the feathers smooth and straight. If you have other breeds of chicken as pets and you have held them, you might have noticed that when you pulled the little sections apart, you could make the feather whole again by brushing the barbules back into the place

On the other hand, the feathers of silkies are different. The name silkies come from the feature of their feathers. They have a very silky texture, hence the name. The texture comes from the absence of small cartilage hooks in each hair of a feather. Due to such absence, the feather becomes silky.

This also indicates that the feathers do not sit straight and the silkies lose the sleek look of the feathers because the hairs do not stick together. The individual feathers wisp around, which makes silkies look furry and slightly messy as well. These birds look like rabbits and many people sometimes refer to them as fluffy slippers with feet.

Moreover, silkies have feathers that grow on their legs and toes. They also have a crest of feathers that looks like a top knot, placed on the top of its head.

ii.   *Feather Patterns:*

Silkies come in regular solid colors most of the time. But there are also certain silkies that have several patterns such as cuckoos, splash, and partridge.

iii.   *Feet:*

Another unique feature of silkies is that they have feathers growing on their feet. This is one of the reasons why silkies should not be allowed to play in muddy areas. Moreover, silkies' feathered feet can become a problem for them if they walk into a non-wired bottom of the cage.

Silkies are recommended to be kept in clean areas and provide a perch for them to sleep on during the night times so that their feathers would stay clean.

If you have purchases silkie primarily as an ornamental chicken or for a show, then you will need to give an extra attention to keeping their feet clean at all times along with their feathers.

iv.   *Toes and wings:*

Most of the breeds in chickens have four toes, while on the other hand, silkies have five toes on each foot. Some are born with fewer toes; oftentimes they have fused or partial toes due to a genetic mutation. Most hatchery-breed silkies are of low quality and most of them have improper toes.

There is no clear and scientifically proven function for the fifth toe found in silkies. And if you are planning on keeping them as a pet, then it does not matter how many toes they have. However, if you have purchased your silkie and you breeding and grooming them for a show, then it becomes a concerning issue. Breeders have to work hard to make sure that their chickens have the right amount of toes, as instructed by the shows, or else, they can get disqualified.

Silkies have a very small body, meanwhile, their toes are medium sized. As mentioned before, silkies cannot sly, hence, their wings do not have a function for flying and they primarily sit far back on the back of silkies.

v.   *Skin, bones, and Meat:*

Unlike most of the backyard chickens which have yellow skin, astonishingly, silkies have black skin. Their skin is quite dark and this is one of the reasons why they are considered to be one of the most popular delicacies in some Asian countries. Silkies have dark grey to black, bones, and meat.

This also makes wonderfully colored. Consider a black colored silkie with black feathers and black skin. This makes them look rich in black color and those silkies appear to be blacker than others. Similarly, the white colored silkie, with black skin underneath, appears to be a deeper color of white.

All these features make silkies more unique and different than the other breeds.

The meat of silkies is also eaten in many countries. Although they do not have a lot of flesh on them, still they are used in many foot items.

It is popularly believed that silkies were originally developed in China. Thus, it has also been seen that the meat of the silkie is used in various foods and especially for medicinal purposes. In China, it is believed that the meat of a silky can help in alleviating postpartum disorders, it helps with menstrual cramps, provides protection against weakness, and decreases anemia.

Moreover, it also increases immunity and works as a treatment for diabetes. But these are all cultural beliefs and there and no scientifically proven claim regarding these properties of the meat of silkies.

vi.   *Combs and Wattles:*

Silkie roosters have walnut-shaped combs. Silkies also have dark purplish -black combs and wattles. This shade is called mulberry. Most of the times, it can be difficult to see the combs and wattles against the black skin of silkies but nonetheless, it contributes to their beauty.

It is common for hatchery birds to have poorly-shaped combs.

vii.   *Face:*

It is quite fascinating to look at the face of the silkies. Once you get a closer look you will notice many features that stand out. The face of the silky is very smooth and it has the same coloring to it; grey and black, like the rest of its skin and feet.

The eyes of the silkies are quite large and they are mostly dark brown to practically black in color. Another feature that is very interesting in silkies face is their earlobes. The earlobes of silkies are in turquoise blue in color. However, if you have a bearded silkie, then it will be really difficult for you to see them.

viii.   *Crests:*

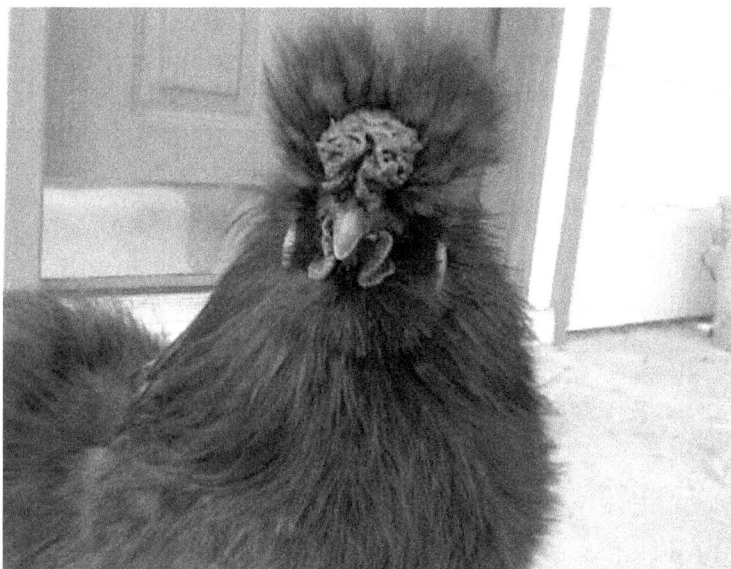

Silkies chickens have a tuff of feathers on top of their heads. They eventually grow out and barely begin to curl around their faces. Their vaulted skull lies underneath this tuff of hair.

Some show chickens and pet silkies have skulls that are arched up at the top of their heads. This also leaves a vulnerable spot for them. Any type of injury or a bullied strong peck on top of their head from the other chicken can cause neurological damage to them or it could actually kill them too.

This is why you should be very careful while handling the silkies and touching the top of their head.

ix.   *Size:*

In general, silkies are a small sized compact breed. They have short legs and roundish bodies. Because of their size and fur like feathers, they look similar to the rabbits. Moreover, the size of silkies varies with country. Silkies in the United States are comparatively smaller than the other counties. They are somewhere between eight to fourteen inches tall.

In other countries, silkies can be found in two sizes. One size is a bit smaller than the ones found in America, while the other standard version of silkies is a bit bigger than the US ones.
Silkies are called bantam, which means miniature chickens.

x.   *Eyesight:*

Most of the time, silkies have difficulty seeing due to their feathery crests and other features of their face. Most of the silkies have their eyes obscured because of such puffy crest.

Breeders of silkies handle this situation in two ways;
  a) The breeders either trim or pluck away the feathers from the face of the silkie, considering the circumstances that the silkies are not needed to be in the show or they don't need to be in that particular appearance where the feathers around their eyes are necessary.
  b) They also opt for another method in which they pin the crest back gently using a hair tie. This is done in a way that does not harm the feathers of silkies but at the same time, it clears their vision and allows them to see properly.

Due to their eyesight, silkies often fall prey to the attacks of predators as they cannot see the area clearly.

## xi.	*Beards:*

**Bearded Silkie	Vs	Non Bearded Silkie**

There are two varieties of silkies
chickens; o Bearded
o Non-bearded

They will be discussed in detail in the later part of this chapter.

There are some silkies that have a group of feathers on their chins,
which appear to be bearded, and then there are that do not have it. It
can be said that it depends on the breeder or the owner of the silkies
as to how they like to keep their silkies. Some prefer the fluffiness
of beards on their face while others do not.

## xii.	*Coloring:*

Silkies chickens come in several beautiful colors such as;
buff, splash, back, white, grey, partridge, and blue colors.

However, if you wish to change the color of your silkie, then
you can color them with food coloring.

However, you have to be extremely careful so that the colors do not harm the chickens and they are safe to be used on animals. This can be a fun time for you and your pet silkie to spend together and bond with each other.

Silkies do vary in their colors. However, it does not affect the physiology or anatomy of silkies.

Moreover, it is worth mentioning here that it is possible to breed different colors of silkies to each other. But it can be difficult to recreate the same colors as of the parents of crossbreeding. It is also not recommended by many experts in silkies.

This is why, silkies are usually bred to the members of the same color, in order to keep the same colors.

Following are the various colors of silkies.

a. White:

White silkie chickens appear wonderful and extremely beautiful. Their whole body looks like it has been covered in the snow including the web, fluff, and the shafts of feathers. The white colored silkie doesn't have any specific markings to determine the sex; either it is male or female.

b. Black:

The black color silkie is quite rich in color. The under color of the feathers is a dull black most of the time.

Their leg matches the colors of their feathers. Black colored silkie's plumage is greenish-black in color and due to their dark black skin, their feathers look rich and magnificent.

When it comes to determining the sex of male and female black silkie, there is very little difference.

c. *Partridge:*

Partridge silkies appear to be sun-kissed in their beautiful color. They are also one of the few silkies that have a significant difference between females and males.

Female partridge silkies are often in mid tone than the males. They have a reddish-bay color and black markings and penciling. On the other hand, male partridge silkies have a rich red color and have a black marking on the front of the neck. The back of the male partridge-colored silkie is green with the markings in green-black color.

Partridge colored silkie roosters have wings that are tipped in black with reddish-bay color. In addition to that, the fluff of the wings is often black with a red tinge. Moreover, the toes and legs of such silkie roosters are black, while the hack is often green-black with rich feathers.

d. Blue:

The blue silkies are essentially in blue slate color. The head of the blue silkie is black and the feathers appear to be quite shiny. The male and female silkies both appear to be similar to each other and there are no differences in colorings or markings between the two sex in order to make a distinction between them.

The hackles of the silkie are in bluish-black slate. The other parts of their body such as; legs, breasts, and neck have the same shade of blue coloring. But there is a presence of black lacing through the feathers.

In blue colored silkies chickens, the tail, saddle, and back are all in the same bluish slate color. In addition to that, there is a presence of shiny black markings on them too.

e. *Buff*

Buff silkies are pure in their color. There are no other markings or a mixture of color on them. They are entirely yellowish beige in color.

This includes their whole body including web, fluff, and the shafts of feathers. Moreover, there is no apparent difference in the coloration or markings between male and female buff colored silkies,

f. *Grey:*

Grey colored silkies are equally wonderful and beautiful. They are often chinchilla grey in color. When it comes to differentiating between the male and female grey colored silkies, there are some slight differences in the markings and colors.

The female grey silkies; hens are often evenly chinchilla grey with slate grey feathers on the head and hackle. Whereas, the male grey colored silkies are in a darker shade of grey with a dark grey head and a light grey hackle with darker grey streaks.

Grey colored roosters have under color in smoky grey shade. Their tail, back, and shoulders are in chinchilla grey. Whereas, the saddle of said roosters match the color of the hackle and the toes. Shanks of such silkies are found to be in slate-blue color.

These are the natural colorings found in silkies chickens.

xiii.   Flight:

As it has already been mentioned multiple times, silkies cannot fly high. Their flight resembles something along the lines of a controlled fall, however, not all silkies can even do that.

It cannot be said that silkies cannot fly at all. They are capable of flying but it requires a lot of energy and most silkies prefer not to put in that much energy.

This is one of the reasons it is always recommended that the breeders should place the perches low in their coop so they can get up and down without having to put a large amount of energy. Moreover, you should be extremely careful while handling the silkies. Be careful not to drop them onto the ground and always set them down gently or else they can get injured or hurt badly.

These were all the prominent physical features of silkies chickens that make them unique and different than the rest of the breeds.

3. Sexing your Silkie

Silkies chickens are considered to be one of the most difficult breeds to sex. Most of the breeders have even said that it could take six or more months to determine the sex of silkies. The reason for this is; both the sex of silkies share many traits and characteristics that could be used to determine the sex in chickens generally. Since in silkies those characteristics could be the same, it can become extremely difficult for the breeders to sex them.

It has been said by many experts in silkies, the older the chicks are, the easier it is to determine the sex. However, there are certain things and distinctive features between hen and roosters in silkies that you can keep in mind while sexing this breed.

- **Hackle feathers:**

The roosters in silkies have a rougher texture to their hackle feathers as compared to the hens in silkies.

- **Crowing:**

This is considered to be one of the best ways to know the sex of silkies. It is determined by the natural trait of males. The silkie rooster starts crowing. Most of the time, they start crowing around the age of four to six months.

It is not exactly proven by anyone but still if you observe the silkie chickens, you will be able to determine their sex.

- **Posture:**

Again, this is not really proven by anyone. But upon looking closer, you will be able to notice that the males in silkies hold their bodies in a more erected manner than the females.

- **Streamers:**

Basically, streamers are feathers that come off of the crest on a silkie chicken. These streamers can only be seen in roosters because females have a rounded crest.

The streamers can be observed in the male silkie chicken around the age of four to six months.

- *Combs*:

The difference between male and female silkies lies in the size of their comb. The female silkies have a walnut comb, and males have a relatively bigger and more prominent comb. This can only be seen if you observe really closely.

- *Guards:*

This is one of the prominent traits of male silkie chickens. From a young age, male silkies adopt the role of standing watch over the entire flock of silkies. They watch over the females in the flocks and try to guard them against any kind of threat or predator.

Moreover, once the silkies start the laying process, it becomes evident which ones are roosters and which ones are hens.

4. Varieties of Silkies

On multiple stances in this book, you came across the types of silkies popularly known as Bearded, Non-bearded, and Bantam. You might be wondering what are those varieties and their characteristics.

In order to eliminate any kind of confusion, let's clear the air with one general fact about silkies. In many countries, silkies are popularly called Bantam Silkies. However, this varies in accordance with the region. According to many breed standards, silkies can be classified as large fowl officially.

Bantam silkie is often considered as a separate variety and its size also differs from one region to another. In America, bantams are recognized, and rarely do we find varieties that are larger than bantams. Whereas, in other countries, the weight varies and there are different standards as well.

While it has been established that bantam silkies have some specific standards and weight set for them, it is also worth noted here that there is no size difference between bearded and non-bearded silkies. Silkies are a smaller breed and all standard sized silkies usually weigh up to 1.8 kgs for a rooster and 1.36 kgs for a hen.

Let's dive deep into the varieties;

1. *Bearded Silkies:*

As the name indicates, bearded silkies have more feathers on their face than non-bearded silkies. They are often the most asked for type in the silkies chickens. Because of their beards they appear to be fluffier than the other type of silkies.

The bearded silkies have feathers that are so soft and silky. They make this breed look like a ball of cotton. They are your typical silkies, which come up when you look for the pictures of silkies.

The silky hair-looking feathers appear that way due to the fact that the bearded silkies do not have any barbicels. The bearded silkies entail both males and females. This characteristic is found in roosters and hens equally. They can also be found in any color that has been recognized and mentioned in the earlier part of this chapter.

The silkie that has a full beard appears to have a muff of feathers that cover the earlobes of this wonderful breed. Those feathers then go around and down the beak and become horizontal. The whole feature seems like it creates a collar. There are also three oval parts in the said area.

Moreover, bearded silkies have a topknot of feathers on the top of their head.

2. Non-Bearded Silkies:

There is not a huge physical difference between the bearded and non-bearded silkies. The only difference is that the non-bearded silkies lack the beard on their face.

The non-bearded silkies are equally soft and have feathers that feel like silky hair upon a touch. They also lack barbicels, exactly like the bearded silkies.

The only difference is that they do not have any beard on their face and their features are more visible due to the absence of feathers that cover the face of bearded silkies. You can clearly see their earlobes which are turquoise. Their face and wattle are also quite visible. Non-bearded silkies have black pigmentation on their face however, they can also be found in all those colors that have been mentioned earlier.

3. Bantams:

However, we have touched upon bantam silkie but let's cover this variety in detail here. In many countries, full sized silkies are often referred as Bantam silkies. Whereas, there are some countries where bantam silkie is considered to be another breed, which is different from other silkies.

There is, however, one difference between a bantam silky and a silky and that is; bantam silkies are often in the actual size of the chicken. Bantam silkies are usually one-fourth to one-fifth the size of a silkie.

Bantam silkies can be bearded or non-bearded and it does not matter which one of the two of these they are, they still vary depending on where they are from, according to the Bantam breed standard.

In the American Standard of Perfection, the bantam silkies are about 1 kg in weight for the roosters. Whereas, for the female bantam silkies, they should be about 907 grams.

According to the British standard for the Bantam silkies, they should be about 500 grams in size for a female, whereas, for a male, bantams should be around 600 grams. Moreover, if we look at the Australian Poultry Standard for Bantam Silkies, the males in this variety should be at 680 grams whereas, the females are at 570 grams.

The aforementioned weight standards are decided upon in terms of their maximum size.

Bantam silkies only vary when it comes to the standard of weight. When it comes to other physical features such as; colors, shape, feathers, they are exactly like the regular silkie.

This chapter entails all that you need to know about the silkies from their anatomy to their physical features, sex, and the varieties that can be found in this wonderful breed of chicken.

Chapter 6: A Guide to Feeding Your Silkie

Silkies are not the most demanding breed in the family of chickens. They eat the same way other breeds of chickens eat. Silkie chickens are in general free ranging chickens.

They roam around and usually collect their food off of the ground or plants. They take things they need like pebbles et Cetra. And this is how they can take care of their own food when they are ranging. However, as a breeder and an owner of silkies, you should provide them with the types of food they eat and can eat in order to ensure their health and nourishment.

This chapter will help you in learning about the types of food your silkies eat and enjoy. In addition to that, this chapter will also give you a few tips in feeding your silkie chickens and the treats you are allowed to give them every once in a while. All of this was mentioned while considering the health and safety of the silkies.

1. *Foods Silkies Can Eat:*

Feeding the silkies is similar to feeding the other breeds of chickens. You don't have to go an extra length in order to get them any special food item. They do not need any different nutrition than the other breeds in the flock. If you have been a breeder to other breeds of chicken, then you don't have to worry at all, but if you are a beginner at owning and breeding chicken and silkies are the first one, then keep reading so that you won't give the silkies something they can't or should not eat.

One thing that should be strictly kept in the mind before getting a feed for silkies is that it should be of top-notch quality. If you are new to owning chickens, it is better to get the feed from the market instead of making it by yourself.

Although silkies are high maintenance chickens, still they need some levels of nutritional goods in order to stay healthy. So, you must be very careful of those things.

The feed comes in three forms and it is highly fundamental for a breeder and an owner of silkies to be in mind to those forms of feed. Those forms are;

i. Crumbles
ii. Pellet
iii. Mash

❖ *Crumbles:*

In crumbles, you get a range of various sizes of grains all in the same pack. Crumbles are considered to be one of the most suitable feeds for the silkies. In addition to that, it has been proven that when silkies are provided with crumbles, they grow in a better way and the laying process also becomes better.

❖ *Pellet:*

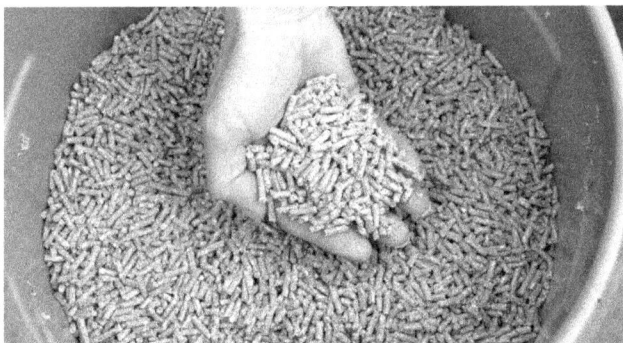

Pellets are also considered really good for the silkies however, they should only be given to the adult silkie chickens and chicks should avoid eating them. They are like any other pellet you would buy for the other breeds of chickens.

Another thing that should be mentioned here, you should always give priority to the crumbles, however, if you cannot find any crumbles then go for pellets.

❖ *Mash:*

When a human baby is around six months, the first feed you start giving to them is mashed food. They can digest it easily and it is best as a starter food. However, adults do not eat mashed food items. The case is quite similar to the silkies.

Mash is the same kind of feed that has a texture of oatmeal to it. You are required to add water to it and then give it to the baby chicks. However, the mash is not really the recommended feed by many breeders for two reasons;

I.   It can get spoiled really quickly
II. It is not the high-quality food

Silkies in general love mash but you should always give priority to crumbles and pellets before mash feed.
These were all the forms of feed that you are allowed to give to your silkies. Now let's discuss the various types of feed that you can purchase from the market to give to your silkies.

- *Starter Rations:*

As the name suggests, starter rations are specially designed for the newly born silkies until they are six weeks old. There are multiple various types of starter rations that come in the market, each varies depending on higher and lower levels of protein present in them. Starter rations also come in a form that has medications already mixed in them. They are a great way to ensure the health of your chick's silkies. This way you can protect them from any type of diseases or illnesses that are commonly found in baby silkies.

Silkies are not meat chickens, which is why you should opt for the ration pack that has a ratio of about 20% protein in it.

- *Grower Rations:*

This comes after the starter rations pack of feed. Grower rations are necessary for silkie chicks that are six to fourteen weeks old. They also come in various levels of protein and again, it is recommended that you should go for the one that has a lower level of protein in it. It is recommended that for a grower ration choose the one with 18% protein in it.

This ration plays its role in helping the silkie chicks get into a great condition for laying eggs.

- *Finishing Rations:*

Finishing rations are what essentially help in initiating the process of laying in the chickens. They are also known as developer rations. Finishing rations have an excellent level of vitamins, calcium, and minerals in them.

They are designed for chickens that are 15 to 22 weeks old. Moreover, while choosing the finishing rations, you should check the protein level in them. It has been recommended that it should have 16% protein in it, not less and not more as it will help your silkies chickens to gain the right amount of weight without getting fat.

- *Adult Rations:*

Adult rations are designed for the silkies that are 22 weeks of age. This is the age where they are given the adult ratio. These are also the type of feed they will be provided throughout their life.

The level of protein in adult rations is usually 16% to 18%. You should always pay attention to the level of protein as it is highly essential for your chickens in the process of laying eggs. Always prefer to purchase the ration from the market as it has various grains and it provides the right amount of feed and nutrients to the silkies.

- *Sweet Feed:*

Sweet feed is a mixture of whole grains or a pallet that is covered with a sweetener such as molasses. They are also known as all stock. It should be kept in mind that sweet feed provides no real nutrients to the silkies and they are more like a treat for them. This is why they should not be given to them on a regular basis as the only feed. It can be harmful to the health of your silkies.

2. How to Feed Silkies?

As a new owner of a silkie chicken, when you learn about the allowed food items that you must give to your silkies, along with it, you should also learn the tips for feeding your chickens. These tips help in contributing to the well-being of your chickens.

As it has already been mentioned in the previous part of this chapter, each silkie's intake of feed differs based on their age. They require different amounts and different forms depending on the fact if they are chicks or adults or whether they have started laying eggs or not. A laying silkie female requires the feed of four pounds for every dozen eggs. Moreover, as an owner, you are supposed to feed 2 pounds of feed for every pound of weight that you want the silkie to gain, considering the fact that they should be healthy and not fat.

Although this seems like a huge amount of feed, this should be kept in mind that you don't have to feed each hen four pounds at every feeding. They might not eat it and the food will go to waste. Give them their required amount of intake.

The required amount of feed for a silkie that has started the laying process is about ¼ pound of feed every day. Both males and females are fed the same amount. You should never force them to eat more than the required amount, this could potentially endanger their health and body size.

Now let's look into the tips you can utilize while feeding your silkies.

1. *Provide Water to the Silkies*:

Silkies should always have access to clean drinking water. It is highly important for them or else they can get dehydrated. You should provide them with fresh water every day. Make sure to clean the waterer on daily basis and keep refilling it multiple times a day.

2. *Let the Silkies Feed on their Own:*

You should feed your silkies twice a day, however, it is also recommended that you leave your silkies to decide their own schedule of feed. Use a feeder and leave the feed in it for the chickens to keep eating from it throughout the day. Silkies often tend to eat in breaks so it is better for them to make their own eating habit.

It is also recommended that you empty out the feeders at the end of the day from the feed that wasn't eaten. Place that feed in a place that is safe from pests as leaving it in the feeder for the whole night could lead mold or pests to grow in the feed and that can endanger the life of your silkies.

3. *The Relationship of Feed with Weather:*

It does sound weird, however, it is true that the change in weather affects the intake of feed taken by the silkies. It has been seen that silkies generally eat more food when it is cold, on the contrary, they tend to eat less when the weather is hot. This is why you should adjust their levels of food with respect to the weather.

4. Provide Your Silkies with Grit:

Silkies are basically free-range chickens. They mostly pick up the pebbles, bones, and things like that while roaming around.

However, if they don't free range often then as a breeder and owner of your silkies, you should provide them with some grit. Grit is essentially a mixture of limestone and granite.

Grit plays its role in helping the chickens to digest their food easily. Without taking the grit, chickens become unable to digest, which can lead to many health problems.

Mostly, young chickens and baby chicks eat a large quantity of grit which can make them skip the feed. This is why, you should be careful as to giving them the grit after they have eaten the normal feed.

Chickens tend to have baths in grit, which can be quite dangerous for their health as it spreads diseases and illnesses. Hence, be careful to offer the grit in a small feeder so that they won't be able to take a dust bath in it.

5. *Introduce Variety:*

It is always welcomed by the silkies if you give them a variety of food every now and then. Giving them a variety entails giving them a treat which can make them stay happy. In the last part of this chapter, you will learn about the different treats you can give to your silkies.

You can follow all the aforementioned tips while feeding your silkies. This will ensure the good health and well-being of your silkie while also providing them with the food of their choice.

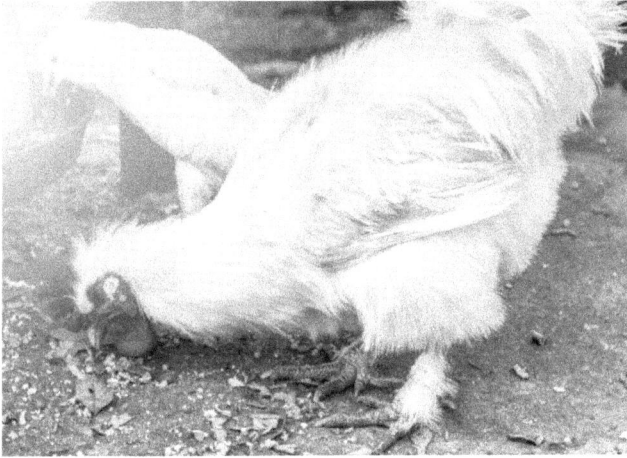

3. A Treat for a Day:

It is important and equally fun to spoil your silkies a little with treats sometimes, however, you should be careful in providing them such foods. Do not make them a staple of their daily diet. Silkies can become picky eaters sometimes, so you have to be careful in giving them the treat in moderation.

Moreover, keep an eye on their health as well. If your silkies start to show signs of diarrhea or indigestion, then put a stop to the treat you give them.

Following is the list of food items you can give to your silkies chickens as a treat.

Treats:	Recommendations:
Bananas	A great source of potassium for the silkies
Bread	Only give this treat occasionally as they are starchy and can become harmful if given in large quantities.
Apple	You can give them in a raw or sauce form, however, be

Silkies: Everything You Want to Know about the Fluff-Balls | 82

of the seeds as they contain cyanide.

Cherries A great treat for the silkies

Rice Always give the silkies cooked rice and never in the raw form. Even when given the cooked ones,

offer them in small quantities.

Flowers Silkies are free ranging birds and when left in the backyard, they tend to eat the flowers. However, you should be careful that the flowers are not poisonous and they do not have pesticides.

Asparagus They can be fed in any form. But

it is better to give asparagus in raw form as it will be easier for them to peck.

Carrots Carrots can be given in any form you prefer.

Broccoli A great and highly recommended treat for the silkies.

Beets Can be given as a whole.

Peppers Only give bell peppers as they are

sweet and never give them the hot

peppers.

Raisins Be mindful in giving them raisins as they contain a large amount of sugar. Only give in moderation.

Cauliflower A highly recommended treat.

Cheese Any kind of cheese can be given. However, it should be kept in mind that cheese can make the silkies fat and when given, monitor the digestion of the chickens as it can induce diarrhea in some of the silkies.

Potatoes Give potatoes in a moderate amount as they also contain a

level of starch. Moreover, it is
recommended to give them in

cooked form, if not, then remove the green part since it can be poisonous.

Lettuce

Any kind of lettuce can be given. They are considered to be one of the best treats and can be given on a regular basis.

Cucumber

It has been recommended that you should give priority to the overripe cucumbers so that the silkies can get access to the seeds as well.

Cereal

Avoid the ones that have high levels of sugar in them. You can offer them the cereals with the least quantity of sugar in them.

Berries

Silkies enjoy berries a lot.

Cabbage

Any type of cabbage is considered a good food item for the silkies. They can also peck it and play around with it as you hang the cabbage in their coop.

Grains

They are an excellent choice for a treat. Some of the most recommended ones are wheat berries, oats, and flax. If given a choice between cereals and grains, you should give priority to the grains while offering this as a treat to the silkies.

Grapes

Feed seedless grapes to the silkies and cut them up so that they won't choke on them.

Peaches

Be careful about the sugar level in peaches. Other than this, they are

	a good treat because of their softness.
Eggplants	Give priority to the overripe eggplants as they are considered to be a great treat.

Corn	You can feed them in a raw or cooked form. They can also eat it off the cob or on it.
Sunflower seeds	They have many benefits. Sunflower seeds can help in the process of laying eggs. Moreover, they help with the development of healthy feathers.
Crickets	They are a great source of protein. Silkies can hunt for the bugs on their own as they free range, or you can get the crickets for them from a pet store.
Mealworms	Similarly, mealworms also have a good level of protein in them. In addition to this, silkies love to eat mealworms. You can get them from a pet store too.
Pears	They are also a very good treat for the silkies. However, you should take care of the seeds and remove them from the pears before giving them to the chickens.
Tomatoes	Silkies love to eat tomatoes and often seek them as they free range.
Melon	In the family of melons, you can give watermelon, cantaloupe, and honeydew to your silkies. They also enjoy the seeds and flesh of the melon.
Popcorn	Make sure there are no salts, oil, or butter on it and they are air-popped.
Squash and Pumpkin	They are quite appreciated by the silkies and they can eat seeds

and
the flesh of both squash and
pumpkin.

Yogurt   Yogurt helps the silkies in
digestion and they can eat both

	regular and flavored ones.
Peas	Silkies love peas and the flower of
	peas
Scratch	Scratch is given during the cold time of the year. They have multiple grains in the, but it should only be given as treat and not the whole nutritional meal.
Pomegranates	They are an excellent treat for the
	silkies.
Table scraps	Table scraps contain a high level of salt and other items that can be
	harmful to the silkies. Give it in a
	very small amount.

Chapter 7: Keeping Your Silkie Healthy: Possible Illnesses for the Silkie Chickens

1. The Necessary Precautions:

Silkies can be vulnerable to various diseases. Those diseases can stem from different sources or by doing things in the wrong way.

As a new owner, you could get confused in the beginning when it comes to many things or you could get overwhelmed and many important steps could slip your mind that can ensure the safety and well-being of your silkie.

Below are the few steps you can take in order to prevent any potential diseases or illnesses from taking place in your silkie.

Step Number 1: Keep the Coop Clean

Raising silkies or any kind of chickens or pets is a huge responsibility in itself. If you are not ready for looking after the silkies and providing them the kind of protection they need, then give yourself some time, educate yourself on how you must take care of them, and then get one. Because the very first rule of keeping them protected is cleaning their coop and disinfecting it from any kind of germs.

You should disinfect the coop on weekly basis and clean it every other day. If the coop is kept clean throughout the week, then the disinfection process becomes easy.

In order to disinfect the coop, wash the entire surface area with soap and water. Once it is dry, wash it again with disinfectant. Leave the disinfectant to sit on the surface for at least 30minutes before washing it off. This will ensure that all the germs, diseases or bacteria are killed. When purchasing the disinfectants, you should give priority to the once that are warm since the warm disinfectants are more effective than the cold ones.

Step Number 2: Keep an Eye On Silkie's Health

One of the most important steps in keeping the silkies healthy is to catch the diseases before they even have a chance to spread in the flock. Look for any kinds of signs. Do a daily health check and if you find any of the silkies lazy, or struggling with digestion or diarrhoea or they are not playing like usual, then immediately take them to the vet and have them checked.

Moreover, in order to prevent the germs from spreading around in the flock, keep the ill silkie in a quarantine.

For the purpose of checking any signs in other parts of silkie's physiology, check if the eyes are bright, their nose and vent are clear of any debris, and if the health of the feathers is well.

In circumstances where the silkies are not showing any kind of diseases or illnesses, then you can let them enjoy and play but it is always important to keep a lookout for them catching any disease.

Step Number 3: Provide Clean Water

Always make sure that the silkies have access to clean and fresh water throughout the day. In addition to this, you should also clean the waterer or the water dishes to make sure that there are no bacteria or germs in the said dishes. When you have cleaned the dishes thoroughly, only then place them out for the silkies to drink water from them.

Moreover, in order to make it cleaner and ensure the safety of silkies, you can also add a small amount of Apple Cider Vinegar to the water. This will help in keeping the pH level of silkies chickens at the required level.

Step Number Four: Keeping the Flock of Silkies Closed

This is a highly important step in minimizing any risks to silkie's health. You should always try to keep the flock closed. The term keeping the flock closed basically means that you do not bring any new, juvenile or adult chicken into the flock, especially without quarantining them first.

Moreover, you should always keep an eye on how the flock interacts with other birds, especially the wild ones. Diseases can spread from one bird to another quite easily, and it is important to reduce the risk as much as possible.

Step Number Five: Make Dust Baths Available

As the name suggests, dust baths are areas or spots of sand or dirt where the silkies can dig in, play around, and dust onto their skin and feathers.

In other words, it is a shower for silkies. It helps in removing many kinds of parasites that may try to leech onto the feathers of silkies.

These were all the necessary steps and precautions you must take in order to minimize the risk of silkies getting any kind of diseases or illnesses. Other than the aforementioned steps, you can also make sure that the feed you are providing silkies with is of high quality.

Moreover, it is understandable how tempting it can get to get carried away with offering the silkies some treats, still, you should be very careful and give them the treat in moderation. Don't offer them the treat daily in order to avoid indigestion and poor stomach.

2. Diseases Common to the Silkies:

Just like any other chicken, silkies are equally prone to some poultry diseases. However, those diseases can be prevented if taken care of or by taking certain safety measures. Below are some of those diseases:

- *Scaly Leg Mite:*

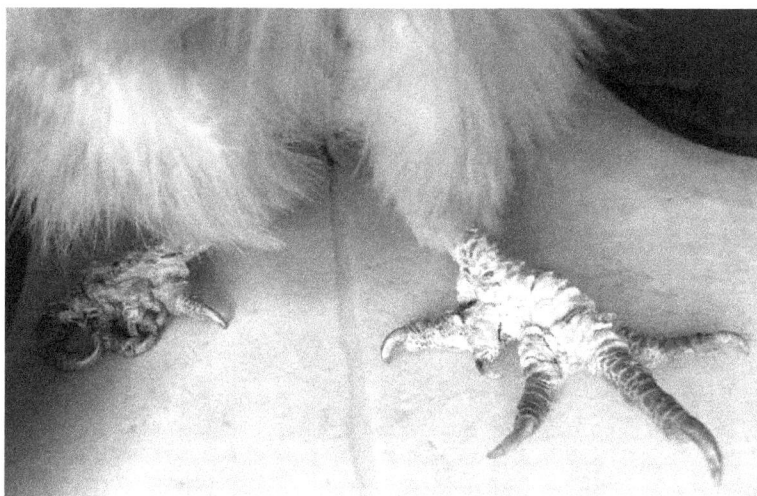

Scaly leg mite or Cnemidocoptes mutans is a parasite that is common amongst silkies. It may be due to the leg feathering, which makes the silkies look more attractive than the ones with clean legs.

In this condition, the chickens start to feel extremely uncomfortable as they get itchy a lot. It is caused by a microscopic mite that burrows beneath the scales of the legs of silkies, raising them and producing a crust that is a mixture of the mites' excreta and skin flakes.

The symptoms of Scaly Leg Mites include:

- o Discomfort in walking
- o Bleeding on the legs
- o Raised leg scales
- o White salt crusts around the legs
- o Swelling in the legs
- o Foot deformation or loss of toes with impairment in circulation

There are certain steps you can take in order to prevent this condition from taking place. Those steps are;

- o Use a good poultry mite powder in order to treat the house.
- o Don't use old-fashioned remedies such as applying diesel or creosote around the house as it can be extremely harmful to the owners and the silkies.
- o Ensure the house is well ventilated.
- o Put some oil like vegetable oil on the perch.

- ● *Marek's Disease:*

Silkies are highly susceptible to Marek's disease. It has been said that the dark eye of the silkie could be one of the reasons why they are prone to this disease. Many problems of silkies chickens are attributed to it and it can be diagnosed only through post mortem of a veterinary surgeon.

Marek's disease is a herpes-type virus, which was first identified by Josef Marek. It infects the lymphoid tissue, causes tumors, and damages the peripheral nerves that result in paralysis of typically one wing or a leg. Twisted or seahorse neck, also known as torticollis may also be present but they should not be confused with water on the brain.

This disease affects most of the system of the body by the interference of tumors with normal functioning such as lesions and tumors in blood vessels and the digestive system of silkies.

This particular infection takes play due to the inhalation of feather debris, as this is where the virus sheds. The virus rapidly spreads all over the body but remains hidden until the symptoms start to appear between four weeks and many months later.

Female silkies are generally more prone to this as it is mostly a result of stress and the hens can get stressed due to the laying of eggs. Moreover, the disease often manifests as the bird comes into lay.

There are certain symptoms you should keep an eye out for;

- A drop in egg production
- Disorientation
- Tumors
- Torticollis
- Paralysis of one wing and one leg, sticking out in opposite directions.

There are some preventive measures you can take such as;

- The silkies should be vaccinated when they are a day old and then again at two weeks.
- Breed for immunity

- It is not highly recommended as mixing species can be dangerous, however, you can bring a turkey because turkeys can carry a certain virus that stops the Marek's virus from producing tumors, and this way the silkies can pick up this virus to kill the already infected one.

- Avoid keeping older birds with the younger ones as the youngsters will pick up any kind of virus. The older a chicken is, the greater its chances are of resisting the virus as chicks are easily vulnerable to the viruses while on the other hand, as they grow old they develop natural resistance from about 5 months of age, which can help them to overcome later infection

.

- ***Water on the brain:***

One of the best silkies considered is those who have a dome on their skulls which produces a crest. However, it can be alarming when noticed in chicks as it appears to be a large bump on top of their head, this could induce panic in new breeders.

It could turn out to be a problem with some of the crested breeds as it is often mistaken for Marek's disease. Infection takes place in the enlarged cranial cavity which produces fluid that in turn presses on the brain.

There are some symptoms that can appear once the silkies get infected by such disease;

o Walking backward
o Falling over
o The silkies might spin around in circles and then abruptly stop

Other than the already mentioned diseases there are also several common diseases that silkies can be vulnerable to. There is always a risk of your silkies getting an infection. Such diseases are;

- Vitamin A deficiency
- Leucosis
- Lice
- Fowl cholera
- Capillariasis
- Avian influenza
- Fowl pox
- Rickets
- Botulism
- Colibacillosis
- Mycoplasma Gallisepticu
- Infectious bronchitis
- Newcastle disease
- Pullorum
- Omphalitis et cetra.

3. Seeking Veterinarian's Help:

New owners of silkies always find themselves questioning the type of veterinarian they should seek for their silkies. This also depends on the type of animal your silkie chicken is. If it is a pet, then you should go for veterinarian care. Whereas, if it is a farmyard chicken, then its care and checkup including the vaccination can be done by the breeder.

You must be thinking, when should you go to the vet for a check up. It is understandable that owners are often reluctant due to the bills and fees of the veterinarian, only to find out that there was nothing serious. At the same time, you want to be cautious and don't want to assume that everything is fine, while the flock could be in a grave condition. In such cases, a single vet visit can help you in understanding such things so the next time you will know when things are serious and when they are not.

As an owner of a pet chicken, you should keep an eye on the birds whenever they start to exhibit unusual behaviors or symptoms. If your silkies start to show any signs of the illnesses, or in general they seem to be fatigue, it is highly recommended that you must seek the help of your veterinarian.

Chickens usually don't require a lot of visits to the vets, still, it is better to check for the illnesses in their initial stage, as some of them are fast working diseases and early detection and treatment can make a huge difference.

It is also worth noted here that the diseases found in silkies or many chickens can be zoonotic. This means that the diseases can be transmitted from the birds to the person or vice versa. This is one of the reasons why you should consider it quite imperative to keep an eye on the health of silkies and getting them checked by the veterinarian.

If you suspect any illnesses or any symptoms of diseases, immediately seek professional help or care from the veterinarian for the silkies.

4. Vaccinating the Silkies:

Before getting into the vaccination tips you can follow, it is first worth mentioning here that not always do you have to vaccinate your silkie chickens. Many people prefer not to due to many reasons. One of the main reasons is creating an organic farm. There are some situations in which you can opt for the vaccination. Those situations are listed below:

a. If the flock is not closed:

In such a situation where the flock is not closed, however, it is strongly recommended to keep it closed in order to prevent any kind of harm to your silkies, an open flock is more susceptible to diseases. Thus, if your flock keeps adding new chickens on regular basis then get them vaccinated, as it will minimize the risk of getting infected.

b. If the diseases are already prevalent in the area:

Find out from the local farmers in your areas which diseases are prevalent and get the chickens vaccinated for only those diseases. There are several diseases that haven't been registered in many areas for quite a while now, which is why you don't have to get the silkies vaccinated for them. Only get the vaccination for the already existing diseases.

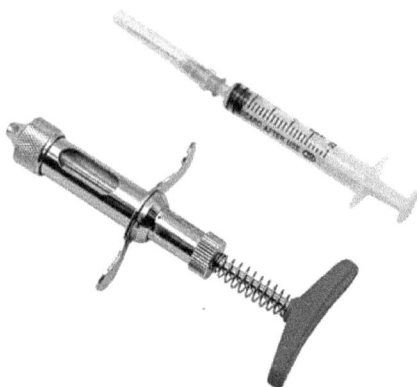

c. If you are purchasing silkies from different breeders:

This is the same as the closed and open flock concept. If you are purchasing your silkies from other hatcheries, breeder, or bird auctions then it is fundamental to get them vaccinated. It is recommended that you should get the silkies from breeders who follow all the necessary safety precautions, yet you can provide extra care by getting them vaccinated on your own.

d. If certain diseases were present in the flock in past:

Make a decision of getting your silkies vaccinated by checking the history of your flock. If there had been a prevalence of any disease or infection in the flock or facility in the past, then you should get the chickens vaccinated for that disease. Otherwise, don't opt for any such vaccination.

e. If the silkies are going to the chicken shows:

You should get your silkies vaccinated in such a situation where you will be taking them to the shows. There will be a large number of chickens present in the same vicinity to each other, thus it will increase the risk of diseases and infections spreading amongst them. This is why get them vaccinated before taking them to the shows. There are some tips you can follow while considering your silkies to get vaccinated. Listed below are such tidbits:

1. Protect the vaccines:

If you are keeping a vaccine at home, then you should store them properly and protect them from heat and direct sunlight. Moreover, keep checking the dates of those vaccines on a regular basis and if found any that are expired or old, then destroy them. Vaccines can deteriorate rapidly and that way they lose their effectiveness.

2. Don't vaccinate sick birds:

Vaccinating an already sick bird does not have any effectiveness in preventing the disease. Hence, never opt for vaccinating a bird that has already been infected with a disease.

3. Vaccinate chicks after 10 days of age:

Except for Marek's disease, in which you are supposed to get the chicks vaccinated within a day of hatching, other vaccinations should not be done before 10 days of age. In this early stage, vaccinations are not as effective.

4. Choose drinking water vaccines:

Opt for those vaccinations that can be given by using the drinking water method. However, make sure the water does not contain sanitizers or chlorine, or such chemicals it as they can kill the vaccine.

5. Take precautions:

Take precautionary measures while handling the vaccine. Always keep in mind that most vaccines have live viruses in them. If you fail to handle them properly, you can expose yourself and the flock to the disease. Moreover, wash your hands and make sure that you destroy or disinfect the vaccine containers after use.

These were all the necessary tips in vaccinating the silkies. There are several companies that provide vaccines for sale. Moreover, veterinarians also provide certain vaccinations but the cost could be more in this way.

Chapter 8: Laying and Breeding

This chapter will cover the laying and breeding process of silkies chickens in detail for you as a new owner to understand the said processes.

1. Layng the Eggs:

Silkies are not known for their laying abilities. They are predominantly ornamental chickens. However, they do lay eggs but it is not as frequent as one would have expected. They produce a small number of eggs in a week. The laying process is also not fixed at a particular number and it could vary depending on multiple reasons. In this section, we will look into all those facts that affect the laying of silkies chickens.

• What could affect the laying process?

If you own a silkie for a show, then the decrease in the laying process may not be a problem for you. But if you are raising it and keeping it for the process of egg laying then you need to keep into account the various factors that can reduce and affect the laying process. Following are the reasons behind the decrease in laying:

a. Disease:

The health of a silkie chicken and the flock can have an effect on the laying process. Several diseases can affect the laying and the decrease in laying is often the symptom of those diseases. This is why you should always keep a check on your silkies' health. It is imperative to catch and immediately kill the disease before it can bring any more harm to laying.

b. Poor Diet:

When silkies are not given a proper diet, the decrease in eggs laying starts to appear and even a cessation of eggs. It is highly important for the health and well-being of the silkies and the process of laying eggs that you must provide the high quality nutrition.

c. Lack of Exposure to Light:

Chickens require a minimum of 14 hours of sunlight a day in order to lay their eggs properly. It can be challenging sometimes since the sunlight during certain climates can be lesser than the rest of the year, and thus, the chickens don't receive the required amount of sunlight.

However, you can help your silkies receive the proper amount of light by providing artificial lighting in the coop of chicken. The type of lighting you use does not matter, but you should make sure that it is bright enough to read a newspaper under it. It should not be lighter or darker than that.

You can set a timer for the silkies to get the 12 to 16 hours of light per day.

d. Molting:

Molting is when a chicken sheds old feathers in order to make new ones. Moreover, during such times, hens rejuvenate their oviduct, which is the organ used in making eggs. Most of the time, the reason for such a thing is the availability of less light in the coop. This happens usually during the winters.

The decrease in the laying of eggs occurs when molting takes place. This means fewer eggs will be laid.

In addition to this, the periods of molting occur more frequently with the age of silkies. The older they are, the more frequently they will molt.

It usually happens at the beginning of winter. In order to prevent it from affecting the laying process, you can use artificial light to slow it down. However, stopping the molting completely is never the option you should go for. When the hens are unable to molt, they start to suffer from poor health and eventually a significant decrease in laying.

You can, however, do one thing; allow molting during the winters of silkie's second year by turning off the artificial lighting in the coop for 6 weeks. In this way, the silkies will molt and the production of the egg will be back to its normal levels after the molt.

e. Stress:

Stress can cause a significant decrease in the process of laying. Stress can be caused by various reasons such as improper handling, not providing them the proper diet, overheating, or moving them frequently.

This can result in a decrease in laying or a complete cessation of production. You can try to keep your silkies feel relaxed in order to prevent stress as it can affect the overall health of the silkies.

2. Breeding the Silkie:

If you plan on expanding your flock, then you will have to invest more time in it. You will be required to start breeding the silkies. The process is not as easy as many expect it to be. There are some procedures that need to be taken in order to produce a baby chick. Before getting into the process of mating and brooding, let's first discuss the important things you should keep under consideration before letting the rooster and hen mate.

While purchasing the silkies you must be aware of the overall health of the chicken. If the chicken has any underlying diseases that can become a challenge in the mating and brooding process, then don't purchase it.

Moreover, the size of the rooster also matters a lot. The bigger the rooster will be, the more chance of producing a chick will be. Bigger roosters tend to be more dominant and healthier than smaller ones. This is why you should give preference to the ones that are bigger in size.

In addition to this, you should also check the age of the silkies you will be placed together in order to mate. While you can breed silkies at a very young, however, it is never recommended to do so. Instead of doing such a thing, breed them when they are around 35 weeks old.

The last thing you should consider while breeding the chickens is choosing by the color and type. If you want to have a flock with the same color, then purchase both hen and rooster of the same color. Similarly, don't breed bearded silkies with the non-bearded ones. They should be bred with the same type.

- *Mating and Brooding:*

After selecting and purchasing the right silkies you plan to breed, it is now time to start the mating process.

When it comes to breeding, it is important to understand that there is a proper timing for it. Several breeders choose to breed chickens during the spring time, while some will breed all year round. This can be done; given that you prefer these two times of the year.

However, it has been recommended that you can also breed the chickens between the months of February and May. During this time, the silkies are in their best health and the mating can be done without any problems.

You can expect a fertilized egg to be laid as soon as the hen has been bred. Some hens lay fertilized eggs for a few days, while most of them lay for up to 3 weeks after breeding. It all depends on the aforementioned factors necessary in the situation of breeding.

When it comes to mating, the only thing you need to do is placing the silkie rooster with the silkie hen or hens in the same coop when you are breeding. Give some time to the chickens to become comfortable with each other for a few days and then the mating starts to take place.

Provide the best nutrition for the hens as they accept mating from the roosters when they have been given a proper diet.

As the time will pass, the rooster will start mating with the silkie hens by climbing on the back of one. It is a quick process as silkies only touch their vents together for the sperm to be deposited to the hen.

You can leave the rooster with the hen or hens if you want to continue the process of breeding. As the silkie hen starts to produce fertilized eggs, she will also begin to brood on the eggs. Brooding is an act where the silkies sit on the eggs that she produces and she can be quite broody, as it was mentioned earlier in this book.

Leave the silkies to brood and hatch the eggs herself, if you want them to hatch. Silkies are an excellent brooder and they can be incredible hatching chickens on their own.

3. The Eggs:

There are a few tidbits you must keep in mind about the fertilized eggs. If properly incubated only then will the egg produce a chick. Moreover, blood spots in an egg do not indicate if it is fertilized or not. In addition to this, you should know that cracking open an egg to see if it is fertile is never an option and you should avoid doing it.

Lastly, it is worth noted here that a fertilized egg can be eaten and there is no difference in taste between an unfertilized egg and the fertilized egg.

It is highly essential for you as an owner to gather the eggs quickly after fertilization. Keep increasing the number of collecting eggs per day. In this way, you can prevent the eggs from getting dirty, which could lead to several diseases. Moreover, an egg will be in a state of suspension if it is not warmed by the hen. Its development takes place after being in incubation.

• *Storing the Right Ones:*

Before starting the storing process, you must collect the right eggs. Check for any cracks or broken shells. If the eggs seem perfect, then you can put them aisde for the purpose of hatching. However, if it does not seem perfect, then you can throw it away. Once you have collected the right eggs, wash your hands because now is the time for you to store them in an appropriate manner.

If you find any dirt on the eggs, wipe it away gently with a cotton cloth and place them in an egg carton with their pointed end facing down.

Chicken eggs can be stored at the temperature of 12 to 15 °C (53 to 59 °F) for up to 10 days before the process of incubation. You should let the eggs sit in this suspended cycle for 24 hours before starting with incubation.

Place the tray of said eggs on a wooden board so that one side is raised and the tray is on an angle. Every day, keep moving the board to a different side of the tray so that the eggs are angled in a different direction. In this way, you will successfully have them incubated.

- *Artificial Incubation:*

Artificial incubation is always an option if natural incubation seems intimidating to you. However, artificial incubation is more time consuming and expensive. For this, you need an incubator, candling lamp, and anti-bacterial cleaning solutions.

Choose an incubator with the proper amount of heat and humidity and the one that turns eggs automatically. You must disinfect it before using it, even if it is a new one. After that, do a test run for 5 hours or more without the eggs.

After making sure that it is running well, let it run again until the heat is at the proper temperature.

Bring out the eggs then and don't place them in the incubator right away. Let them warm up to room temperature. Mark them "O" and "X" on the opposite sides so that you would be sure that the eggs are being turned regularly.

Place the incubator in an area with constant temperature and then place the eggs in the incubator. Keep checking them and don't add new eggs until after the first batch of eggs hatches out. Moreover, don't breed different breeds simultaneously in the same incubator as the time of hatching varies in different breeds.

You can check the eggs by the use of a candle to determine how developed they are. If found any being infertile, then you can throw them away. By the 21st day, the chick will be ready to hatch from the egg.

4. The Hatchlings:

Silkie hens are known for being the most amazing mothers. It would be better for you to leave the silkies in the care of their mothers as they will keep them warm.

However, if you are raising them without hen, then you will need a ceramic heat lamp with a ceramic bulb for the purpose of heat and light. Never subject new chicks to artificial light, instead use natural light and darkness.

When you hear piping from eggs, which could be heard in the 18th day, turn on the heat lamp and the temperature under the lamp should be 39 °C or 102 °F. Once they are hatched, leave them to dry for a few hours. When they are completely dry, take them out and make sure that there is a waterer in one corner, so the chicks can get water.

Another thing that is worth mentioning here does not place them on a perch as they can easily get seriously injured by falling from it. You can feed them the feed and rations as mentioned in chapter 6. However, you should know about the factors involving in vaccinating the hatchlings.

- *Vaccinating the Hatchlings:*

Vaccination should be under certain scenarios which were mentioned in chapter 7. If you are keeping a small flock in the backyard and keeping it organic, then you do not have to get them vaccinated.

If there is a prevalence of disease in your flock, then get them vaccinated or if you are bringing new chickens then it is necessary for the silkies to get the vaccination.

Most of the times vaccination are done on chicks for Marek's disease. Other than this, it is not necessary to get them vaccinated for every disease. Discuss with your local breeder in order to find out what vaccinations you should get for the silkies and chicks.

Chapter 9: General Facts about Silkies

Below are one of the most interesting facts about silkies chickens;

1. Silkies are one of the oldest known domestic breeds of chicken. They have been known for many hundreds of years.

   Marco polo during his travels in Asia wrote about silkies in the 13th century. He described them as furry chickens with black skin. It is safe to assume that silkies have been around for at least thousand of years.

2. When it comes to the lifespan of silkies, they are one of the longest-lived breeds. Silkies have a life expectancy of around 8 or 9 years.

They also remain productive relatively longer than the other breeds. They keep laying eggs even after most breeds stop. The reason behind it could be their low productivity rates and docile nature.

3. Silkie hens are known for their broodiness. They can brood longer than any other breed. In fact, it has been said that silkies can raise three in a year quite easily. Moreover, they can also sit the eggs of other birds and can brood them into hatching.

4. Silkie chickens' crests are larger than most breeds. Some of them have beards as well, as was discussed in detail. Their feathering makes them look much fluffier and bigger than other chickens.

5. Silkie roosters hardly ever crow. It cannot be said that they never crow, however, they are pretty quiet. This is one of their unique characteristics as it can make them ideal for suburban backyard farms, where neighbors could object to the noise. Moreover, their temperament is quite calm and friendly.

Even when they are startled, they don't make any loud noises, unlike other roosters that crow loudly at the smallest of sounds.

Silkie roosters also do not attack the humans like the other breeds do. In fact, it has been seen that they rather run away if they are provoked.

6. One of the most interesting rumors about the origin of silkies have been spread by some Dutch breeders, who seem to believe that silkies are a result of cross between chickens and rabbits.

PICTURES OF SILKIES GROWING UP

Silkie chicks in incubator

One day Old Silkie Chicks

Three day Old Silkie Chicks

Three to Five days old Silkie Chicks

Week old Silkie Chicks

7-10 Days Old Silkie Chicks

Three Weeks Old

Four to five weeks old Silkie Chick

Five to six weeks old

8 to 10 weeks old

12 weeks old

14 weeks old

16 to 18 weeks old

8 years old silkie rooster

www.ingramcontent.com/pod-product-compliance
Lightning Source LLC
LaVergne TN
LVHW051130080426
835510LV00018B/2331